The Woman, The Love, The Death

To Josh, who inspired every happy poem and continues to.

To Macee, for being the most light-filled supporter.

To Jesus, for giving us the opportunity to see the ones we care about again.

Trigger Warnings:

Mentions of abuse, depression, death and themes of suicidality. Take care of yourself <3

Contents

The Woman, The Love, The Death
                                    1

Foreword: 9

Part One: The Woman Who Learned
                                   11

Childlike Innocence   12

depression   14

messes are mine   16

Only a lil   17

Anger So Pretty   19

practice compassion   20

Silence can be the loudest 21

Christmas Goodbyes   24

Heavenly jewel   27

acid rain   31

maybe I'm a good person even if you're
not   33

Peaces or Pieces   36

Wilted, Jilted and Jaded   38

RAGE   39

Burnt Out   41

To live in love?   *42*

Part Two: To Love   *45*

     Happy days note   *46*

     Find me   *49*

     Hearth is Warm   *50*

     Coffee with a Friend   *53*

     To Be So Cold   *55*

     secret heights   *57*

     Your mind says you are not worth it, but I disagree   *58*

     The blaze   *61*

     Two Can Make   *62*

     the effects of the before   *64*

     Thorns   *67*

     Ease into oblivion   *69*

     home   *71*

     rings and plans   *73*

     I love you!   *74*

Part Three: Even with Death Impending   *77*

     Where it all began   *78*

Forever coveted   *80*

The Monotonies   *81*

the sounds of mourning   *83*

you were too good for life84

the lace of death   *86*

Give Me You   *89*

Leave me   *91*

Our last moments   *93*

Foreword:

Let them be confused

For these strung up words

Are but a muse

Like a tangle of cords

Maybe meant to amuse

A swell of letter hordes

Meant to accuse

Let them be confused

For these sentences

Are but a mindless fuse

Enrapture the senses

The jumbles of use

Might require a consensus

If one tries to construe

Part One: The Woman Who Learned

Childlike Innocence

It's over

Childhood laughter

Colorful joy

All broken with my old toys

It's over

Sterling memories

Thrill of life

Traded for a soul of strife

It's over

Sunkissed daydreams

Future so bright

Potential scared by my fright

I waste away

Day by day

Wishing  that I could just play

My hands aren't my own

My mind no longer a home

What if I just let go?

I don't want to fight

Settle the scores of my own plights

Painfully grasping to avoid heights

I'll stay in this in between

Praying for joy to glean

depression

a dark cloud hovers

twinging in a head

sometimes wish to be dead

huddled under the covers

rainy days

lighting fades

holding onto charades

fanning the cloudy haze

don't forget the better times

a place where you can laugh

grasp the remembered photographs

make the futuristic joys chime

comparison is exploration

so you know the way to go

maybe one day there'll be an outgrow

leading to honest edification

you must know what light is

to actively avoid the darkness

messes are mine

i don't want to regress

but i miss the comfortability of being a
mess

i'm unreasonable

yet in my mind these things are feasible

late night thought spirals

maybe i should write them in my faded
spiral

i'm in therapy

maybe one day i'll be free

find me where the trees

meet the sea

a roaring waterfall in my mind

are all the screams only mine?

Only a lil

I'm feeling　　　　a lil hazy

　　　　　　　My thoughts are dazy

　　　　Found you in the street

　　　　Looking a lil out of sleep

　　　Run your way through town

　　　Maybe we find a lot thrown out

Life gets a lil tolerable

When you start to feel a lil taller

Keep the race going

With your thought pace slowing

You can do this, I know

Give the others a show

It's ok to give in

When time has come to an end

Anger So Pretty

A delicate face

A hardened scowl

A raised brow

I've never been flimsy lace

A twinge of disgust

Red lips sneered

Harsh words revered

My rage flows like a gust

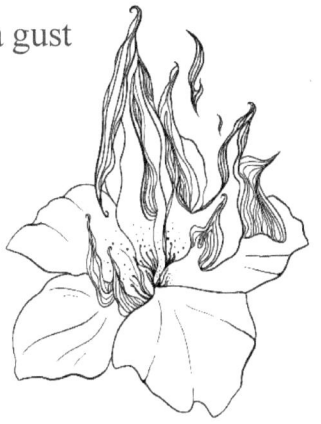

I'm more than you
think

Not just poetry
and paints

Get inside my head

You'll learn I'm more than you're being fed

practice compassion

I WOULD LIKE TO SCREAM

BUT I'M A LITTLE TOO MEAN

to myself

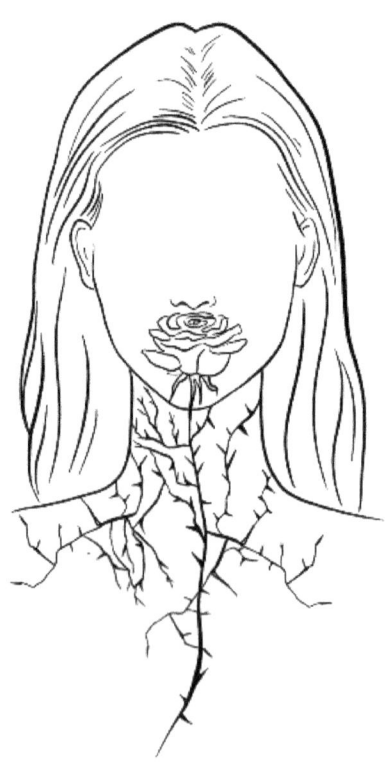

Silence can be the loudest

Shadows cast through a windshield

I take out a bottle of pills

Deep talks while holding back tears

An indie song plays on

We face our mortality

And our parents' spirituality

We're sitting for a while

Both feeling tired

It's worth the exhaustion

To further our connection

Soft words are a pathway

Delicate touches a progression

Cool air providing a sensation

My thoughts, a hopeful manifestation

The clock is still flipping

We come to a mutual understanding

To settle down our yearning

You take your leave

As my car dings

Blowing a kiss

The street lamps illuminate your slip

The door  slams

And

magnifies

silence

A deep breath to still my soul

I turn the volume up

Without your hand to touch

The sound fills the space you once occupied

Now my soft utterances

Becomes calming sighs

And it's time for me to move on

I hope you sleep well

Without my thoughts in your head

Maybe I'll sleep too

But only to thoughts of you

And how you looked under

The shadows casted through my windshield

Christmas Goodbyes

Lights were strung on trees

The air filled with memories

You smiled at me

I stopped by to say hello

Like the lattes we drank

My heart was toasty warm

Thoughts rolled off the tongue

Like a light rainstorm

Oh, What a tainted memory

Who would've thought

I haven't seen you in so long

I texted you on Christmas Day

Hoping that you hadn't gone your own way

But you know what they say

To let loose what you love

Because it's better to be alone

Then to be leading someone astray

But I can't let myself slip too far away

A hallmarked past

A walk through the park

Who could've known

We'd never be able to stay

My heart is frostbitten

And I left the swings feeling lost

I wish you had just told me

That you didn't wish to be my family

I would've understood

Had you just let me stand where you stood

I could've supported your every wish

Instead of begging for you to miss this

Because I thought we had good times

Your eyes twinkled brighter than the lights

Maybe I was wrong

Or maybe you were only putting me on

The funniest thing is

I wouldn't take our fondness back

For sometimes it's okay

To leave joy in the past

I still wish you the best

Even if we both left

Heavenly jewel

You always liked to paint

Landscapes and album covers

And I liked to the ways your colors reflected
on me

You always cared about others

And their internal struggles

Always protesting for the weaker man

Writing songs about overthrowing the
government

I was with you

In the landscapes you painted

Watching sunrises lay upon you

You shone the sun on me

You heavenly jewel

I saw your reflections

You cared about my secrets

And the pain inside my mind

I was the weaker man

You were throwing down the barriers

You heavenly jewel

I saw your reflections

But then you turned insidious

Cutting me down

And painting me grey

Did I ever truly see your refractions?

You heavenly jewel

Your reflections are fading

I can see you value yourself over all

And hate those who don't live for your shine

I hope you get better

But you'd have to live up to your namesake

I hate to wish you could live up to my
expectations

You heavenly jewel

Now my light is reflecting on you

Because in the end

I learned you only liked to paint

Yourself as the ever-delicate victim

To manipulate those

Who were clouded by your charisma

Distracted by your next grandiose vision

You heavenly jewel

I see you clearly now

You're just a bit of rock

And I broke it off now

acid rain

I stand watching from the limelight

Dazed in this bright light

Wouldn't you carve me out of stone?

Etched on your face, a love longing gaze

Silently weeping through this haze

Wouldn't you face my pain?

I reach out
tepidly,
trying
hopelessly

while you
fade away
slowly

Why
won't this
vision save me?

Forever basked in acid rain

My tears flow through the streets

Right down to your feet

Please don't splash me

maybe I'm a good person even if you're
not

is it mental illness or toxicity

i guess it's not really up to me

either way i'll aim to please

don't forget about me

manipulation and degradation

fuels my inner self-esteem

you want me to be perfect

don't worry, i live to appease

baby please

don't forget about me

i want my own legacy

probably based on your ideologies

people suck at seeing me

that's expected

when i can't find my own identity

what do I know

what do I like

other than creating art

what's my existential crisis today

other than obeying your way

i'll lend you a helping hand

hopefully you'll find it grand

i always gave you my best

and abuse is the only thing I get

i hope you find a therapist

and you really try your best

i know you love

but it's less than my sum

if I could've, i would've continued giving

but where's the line between my self-
preservation

and being your encouraging support system?

don't forget I always wanted to be there

i just couldn't be torn down more

but i once thought you were worth it

 I was told to value myself too

Just know, I'll always remember you

Peaces or Pieces

Oh, you with your words

So, unlike my love

Holding my heart in pieces

Give me my slivers

Oh, why can't I wake up

I'm screaming

Shockingly sinister

I'm hardly breathing

My mind is a wasteland

your scarred hand

Slaughtered the peaces

and turned me into ashes

Willing you to hear

All you have to do is bend your ear

Now I know what to accept

How to be held as I feel inept

I'd fight you to the death

As I've learned to treasure my breaths

Wilted, Jilted and Jaded

Wilted, jilted and jaded

My love for you only faded

Each strike of a barb

Only meant to harm

Left me feeling confused

And overtly used

Wilted, jilted and jaded

My blooms only capitulated

Fluttering down, down, down

I'm now only brown

No color left to my beautiful bloom

Just sticks created from doom

RAGE

I've kept my rage contained

for as long as I've had the mind to do so

It sits in a jar in my stomach

Making a ruckus

It bubbles and bubbles

until it bursts through the top

Going all the way up

Until it won't stop

It flows into my mouth

And rarely ever spills out

But this time it spews

Onto 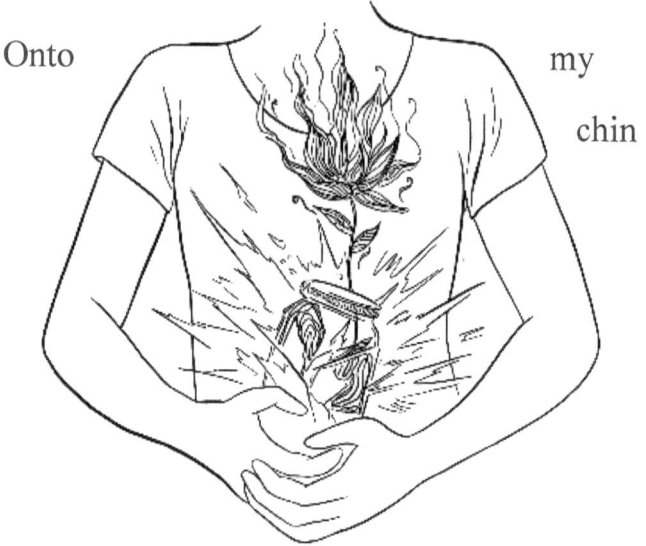 my

chin

And all over you

Burnt Out

I've given you all my wits

Been charred for far too long

Cause you burnt the love out of me

You scuffed me out with your boot

And you can't take more out of a pack

Cause I'm all you have

I'm down to my last end

And I won't be on the mend

Cause I'm burnt out on loving you

To live in love?

There will come a person
Who loves you innocently
With pure intentions
and without rejection

The kind of person who thinks benevolently
And wonders for ways to make life easy

A lover who fights for you
And shields your heart in a battle

When push comes to shove
You stumble right into love

Cause no one compares
To the one you never want to share

They help you not overthink

The things that chink your armor

They weld your heart together

And meld the holes that made you sink

Your malleable heart won't break

When it's time to decide your fate

To live and love?

Or love in death?

Part Two: To Love

Happy days note

Little fishies in bubbling seas

Sunny blue skies to watercolor

I write "I love you" in a little letter

These are my happy day notes

Blaring throwbacks in my sedan

Seeing a long-lost friend

Maybe I'm not so depressed

The evidence of a happier day

Is stored within my soul

But tangible proof is helpful

To cure my aching psyche

So I take the time to describe

My positive feelings

In a little writing app

So I can look back

To remember

life isn't always only bad

Little fishies in bubbling seas

Sunny blue skies to watercolor

I write "I love you" in a little letter

These are my happy day notes

Yellow daisies flowing in the wind

Calling up a beloved friend

Books to read about hope

I put these all in my happy days note

Keep encouraging me

Remind me of the joy that is yet to be

If I was happy once before

Surely I can be happy once more

Find me

Find me under the willow trees

Peacefully sowing all my seeds

Find me wrapped in warmth

Disguising all that which comes forth

Find me on an empty porch

Grappling for any thing of sort

Find me soaking up the sun

Listening to the soft sounds that run

Hearth is Warm

We were once blazing trails

Spurned by the world

Scorching the love, we'd try to hide

It was a long, long road

Full of tales and woes

We'd always meet up

at the crook of the bend

Scraping dirt from our hands

More than small embers

Flames flicking higher and higher

Too volatile

We'd leave it all

Out in the dust

Years go by

The time flies

I still think of you

Even when I don't want to

But I welcome it

When your eyes meet mine

Here in this new time

Don't let it go

I still know who you are

It no   longer scalds me

Meeting you here

Where we've
worked through our
fears

Not burning our tears

The hearth is warm

Less than a
simmer

Now less bitter

Keep it up

Move to a hug

Cozy and bright

The hearth is warm

Coffee with a Friend

Coffee with a friend

We're both on the mend

Sipping up secrets

Total appeasement

Smile with dimples

It is so simple

Milky Rosetta

With a spot of ease

Loving contentment

Zero resentment

Being fully known

Always right at home

Comfortableness

Within our messes

Coffee with a friend

We're both on the mend

To Be So Cold

It's getting kinda cold in this storm

I'm trying to find someone warm

Everybody else has someone to hold

While I'm stuck in the frigid snow

They say wait to stir up love

Until love so desires

But what is it called when I alone

desperately desire

Someone to defrost my soul

Cause I'm too cold

To be here all alone

It's 70 below

And I'm wearing all my clothes

My heart is on my sleeve

Cause it freezes more inside of me

I want your arms to wrap around my waist

To cure this weathering ache

I can't wait any longer

To deny myself this fire

Cause I'm too cold

To be here all alone

Be still my soul

Wait for a heart of gold

secret heights

private lovers

tangled covers

silent pleas

on your knees

shattered walls

caress then fall

lift you higher

how much it matters

panting breaths

smiled secrets

trace your skin

let's meet again

***Your mind says you are not worth it, but I
disagree***

Things got tough

You said, "I'm not good enough"

But you know your life has been tainted

I try to keep

You swimming upstream

But the waves knock us down easily

Grasp your hand

To search for our pined homeland

You wonder if our near end is fated

But I've been there too

Here, let me hold

Pull you into my arms incontinently

My darling

You are my foretold everything

My hopeful thoughts become your privy

Cause you'll say

Baby don't love me that way

I find it all a little too strange

I'll make a way

To aid in your stay

When life begs you to run away

Then you'll see

What your spirit means to me

I'll confirm your worth won't change

Believe me now?

Your existence wows

We can keep our losses at bay
Cause I'll say
I love you that way

I'll find a way
To aid in your stay
When life begs you to run away

Tears in your eyes
Your head won't hold more lies

I thank God
Our minds let us hold on to awe
We both fight for love to stay
I look forward to the rest of our days

The blaze

And I would walk through fire

Just if you were   tired

To love is to   burn

Before   tides

turn

Crash into me

With all your self-esteem

I'd love even if I was all alone

Two Can Make

Oh, the trouble two can make

The promises that'd break

Where the wind will lead

Won't you follow me?

Can be thick as thieves

Won't put you through a sieve

I will make it worth your time

Long as you promise you're only mine

Carve it on a slab of stone

Hang it on every post

That you're mine, mine, mine

Oh, the trouble we will make

All the promises we've made

the effects of the before

Do you get nostalgia

When my hands are on ya?

Do you think of a lovers' past touches

When our cheeks heat in synchronized
blushes?

How come every time you sigh

I die a little inside

Cause your fond memories

Are my haunted dreams

The people that make you an experienced
lover

Make me scared to pull you tighter

I'm new at this

All these feelings and expectations

Are driving me mad

When can I
ever measure
up
To the
women
you used
to love

And I'd brag about you all the time

But I can't find the time

To stop remembering your used lines

The hands that used to hold you

Like I try to do now

The unknown sweet little nothings

That made someone else feel something

I know you'll find a way

To make our love a cliché

As long as it's as new to you

As it is to me

I'm giving you my heart

To make it your favorite work of art

Maybe ours will beat as one

Fueled by our own love

Thorns

My skin is riddled with barb wire

Twisting and curling up my arms

Onto my hands

It grew into this thorny cage

Because I liked it better that way

It gives me a reason

To keep my distance

Sometimes you push your luck

Trying to find a way to touch

Me gently and softly

But that caress was once one of violence

And now I can't tell the difference

Between a harming clutch

And a light loving touch

I know it wasn't you

Who had hurt me in the pursuit

But my mind only knows that hands are hands

Not if they belong to my homeland

Ease into oblivion

No one else gets the privilege
To ease you into oblivion

That right is reserved for me
And our subtle tranquilities

Breath hovers in my mind
Heart beats intertwined

Preserve this bliss
Seal the deal with a kiss

Toy with your messy strands
Let's meld all our plans

Lacing our fingers

Your scent lingers

Burn out our wits

With every touch of our lips

Home

Like nostalgia that moves you to tears
The familiarity calms all your fears

Winding and long is the road home
After you've had time to roam

A constant melody fills your head
While you ponder in your bed

It's a smoldering fire
And a book that never tires

Like a hug from an old soul
Home is where you can grow

It's a porch light left on

And a welcome greeting

Find warmth in the place you know

Home can be where you sow

rings and plans

Sparkle in your eyes

Maybe I could make you mine

Color 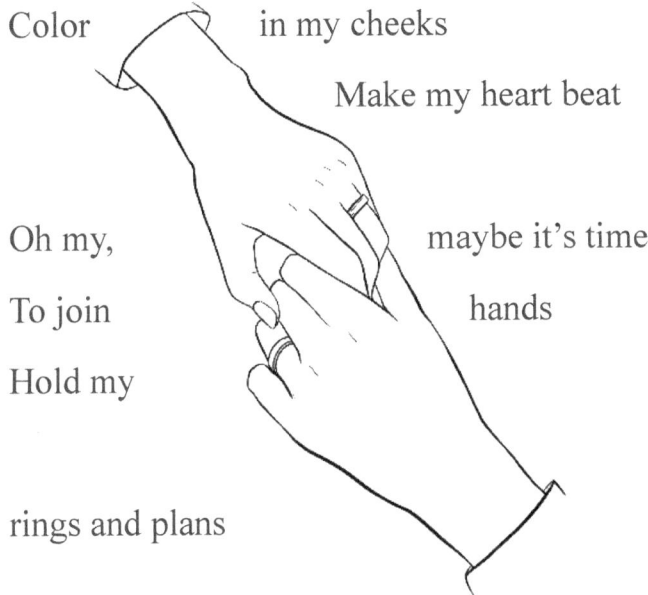 in my cheeks

Make my heart beat

Oh my, maybe it's time

To join hands

Hold my

rings and plans

I love you!

Your smile is mine

You gaze in loving softness

As our faces fit the screen

Our eyes connect in sweetness

Your smile gave a gleam

The light warms our faces

Our love heats our heart

Soon I'll be in laces

And we'll be a work of art

From the beginning

I've prayed for this day

Your smile was my unending

Forever is headed our way

Your eyes are a gateway

Into our blissful future

The blue is truly my favorite hue

I'm amazed, I love you!

Part Three: Even with Death Impending

Where it all began

Hiding in an alcove

Waves crashing on the coast

Wheat weeds flowing

Slow breeze blowing

Nobody knows you

as the dirt do

Sun beams reaching

Children dreaming

Docking in a place

Where nobody knows your name

Inside aching

No more hating

Erased pollution from your mind

Stretching timelines to be kind

Reflections judging

Introspective hugging

Flickering city lights

No one to hold us tight

Beloved wondering

Escape from stumbling

Soothing repetition

Rearview coalition

Going to a secret place

To be free and safe

Air-vents warming

Secluded evening

Guardrails split up

Difference between hate and love

Waves crashing on the coast

In a hidden alcove

Forever coveted

And when the aches of my pains

Take away the love for the game

I'll still journey there in my mind

Grasping onto that far away time

When we moved freely through life

Without much thought to
oversight

It will all fade away

As time always says

But you my beloved

Will forever be my coveted

Whether I stand, sit or lay

I will love all our days

The Monotonies

I feel your caress linger like an uneasy breath

As I lay in bed, our hands interlace above your head

One of us is fading and I wish it was me

You deserve to exist in this life moving forward

What did I do to deserve another breath?

Did I steal it or did you gift it to me?

What  about all

these

inconsequential
monotonies?

The sound of you stirring your hot coffee

The touch of lips on my forehead as you disappear for your day

The warmth from your thumb as you cradle my face

the sounds of mourning

drip, drip, drip

my tears fill the floorboards

of my dreary foggy mind

sip, sip, sip

from the coffee

that I'll now always miss

shine, shine, shine

The sun invades our blues

I miss you

you were too good for life

i remember that night too vividly

shallow breaths, the last one

sobs of sorrow, panicked joy

drip, drip, drip

the grief consumes through the years

like a leaky faucet filling my tears

as your heart faded,

mine palpitated

it can't be true

my life without you

your childlike wonder returned

in the hours you moved on

until your muscles shriveled

and your life chased the ending dawn

the lace of death

what a brave declaration

of such fond adoration

the dirt buries your elation

i toss a handful for retribution

the sun always fades

in light of your passing face

the edge of black lace

covers the tears of a past age

from life to death

and dirt to breath

a budding wreath

born from defeat

Death wraps you in her arms

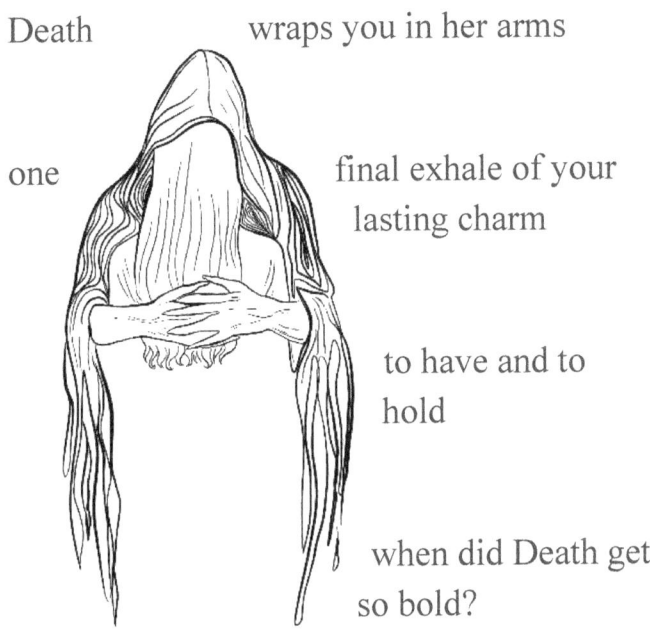

one final exhale of your
lasting charm

to have and to
hold

when did Death get
so bold?

She greets you with a tear

from a place you once called dear

let your own grief swell

for your loved ones know it well

well wishes splash

into a fountain of salt

Death requires a payment

for her pride to be bought

Give Me You

From the hollows of my bones

To the depths of my soul

You call me home

Every ache and pain

Is but a passing thing

Oh God, give me you

Every breath I long for

Return to you

Let my lungs fill up with your sweetness

Let me find you in this lightness

Every harrowing thought

Cursing my whole life

Give me one goodbye

I will hang by this thread

Clothed in your righteousness

Give me all your love

That I may spread it all

All for you

Leave me

And when the day comes

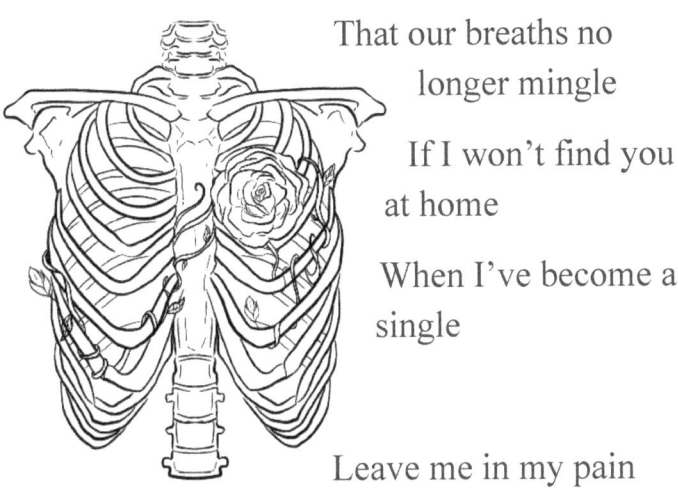

That our breaths no
longer mingle

If I won't find you
at home

When I've become a
single

Leave me in my pain

When the day comes

That your eyes won't meet mine

Your laugh won't light my soul

Or your thoughts impress my mind

Leave me in my pain

Let me have the day

That I grieve my truest friend

To be wretched and lay

Life goes on, but it would be the end

Leave me in my pain

Until I turn grateful for the memories

And I've become once more sane

Til I love to hum your vintage melodies

To soothe my rawest pains

Our last moments

And when my death occurs

I know it will be worth it

To have thought of your soul

In my last moments

About the Author

Mattie Paige finds thrill in writing evocative poetry pieces showcasing typically unmentionable emotions and lived experiences. Mattie has a BS in Psychology and is currently working towards her Masters in Social Work. In addition to this debut poetry collection, she is set to be published in Wishbone Magazine come November 2025 for her flash nonfiction piece titled, "My Good Friend, Death." In addition to writing, Mattie enjoys reading romance novels, listening to music, and hanging out with her husband and mini labradoodle.

Want to learn about upcoming projects?

Check out my Socials:

Instagram: @authormattiepaige

TikTok: @authormattiepaige

Praise for The Woman, The Love, The Death

"The Woman, the Love, the Death is honest and raw, willing to delve deep into topics that others avoid. It'll hit with darts of wisdom and vulnerability that hurt so good because they're true."

-- Mary K. Gowdy, author of "Leftover Thoughts", and "Where Have We Come From, Where Are We Going?".

www.ingramcontent.com/pod-product-compliance
Lightning Source LLC
Chambersburg PA
CBHW051640120626
46551CB00014B/2149